AMIT KHAIRA

WHEN SCREENS GO QUIET

7 evidence-based steps for helping your child readjust, reconnect and flourish.

NXTMOVE

For permissions or inquiries, contact:
NXT Move Plus 8 Ltd
Email: amit@nxtmove.global

First Edition: 2026

Early readers reflect...

"I know Amit and his heart for young leaders. This book is about taking the opportunity to invest in a generation helping them become a force for good. Parents, educators, and youth workers will find this a helpful guide to navigate these new times, assisting young leaders develop new and positive habits. Can't wait to put this into practice!"

Keith Cote
// Global Summit Next Gen Lead Global Leadership Network

"When Screens Go Quiet is a timely and deeply humane guide for parents navigating one of the most consequential shifts of our time. Grounded in careful research yet written with compassion and hope, Amit explores what becomes possible when the constant noise of digital life finally recedes. In that quiet, families are invited back into presence - into shared attention, real places, and the formative experiences that shape resilient, grounded children. Free of panic or blame, this book offers practical wisdom and a hopeful vision: that healthier rhythms, deeper connection, and renewed wonder are still within reach when we make space for life beyond the screen."

Mr Chris Elisara, Ph.D., MBA.
// Director of WEA Sustainability Center; WEA Special Envoy for Environment, Climate & Cities; Founder and Executive Director, Creation Care Study Program; Faith for Cities Executive Director.

"My friend, Amit Khaira has written a very useful guide to help parents, mentors, and educators navigate the challenging new world of technology today. This is one aspect of modern living that many of us would appreciate some guidance in. The creative design of the book makes it easy to read and the practical ideas given makes it easy to apply. As I was reading through the book, I was constantly asking myself: *"That's a brilliant idea. Why didn't I think of that?"*. I highly commend this useful book for your personal reflection and application. Amit, you have done it again!

Ps Benny Ho
// Leadership Mentor - FCC

"As a child and adolescent psychiatrist, I found *'When Screens Go Quiet'* both timely and essential. This book not only unpacks the research behind Australia's social media ban, but also provides invaluable guidance on supporting children's development during these transitions. It's a must-read for navigating how to help children thrive with resilience in the digital aftermath".

Dr Kiri von Klier, MD
// Clinical Research Lead - Mental Health, Innovation Consultant, South Metropolitan Health Service

"Amit Khaira has written an important and thoughtful book on raising children in an age of social media. As a parent and practitioner, Amit gives clear guidance to making good choices."

Dr. Mac Pier
// Founder - Movement.Org

"*When Screens Go Quiet* is a valuable and encouraging resource for parents. Through solid research, practical advice, and insightful reflections, it supports families in creating deeper connections that will help their children flourish. These are challenging times that parents have not had to navigate in history, so I highly recommend the work of Amit in creating a resource to strengthen parents today".

Letitia Shelton
// Author, Founder - Disruptive Women

It's great to see you here!

This guide was inspired by the world's first national social media ban for under-16s, implemented in Australia...a cultural shift that sparked new conversations about wellbeing, identity, and resilience. The following insights, research and reflections aim to support families, educators, and communities everywhere as we navigate, in these early days of the law being implemented, life beyond constant connectivity.

Drawing on global social media trends, generational research, eSafety insights, and cultural-faith perspectives, this resource offers practical ideas and hopeful rhythms you can adapt in your own context.

Our hope is that these pages encourage you to pause, reflect, and try simple practices that bring calm and connection into everyday life. Explore the reflections, try the suggested actions, and share the journey with others.

Together, we can help the next generation grow with confidence, resilience, and hope, while restoring balance and belonging in our homes and communities.

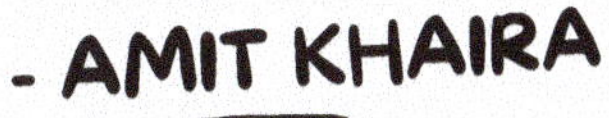

- AMIT KHAIRA

Contents

To Skye,
My greatest editor in love and life, thank you for your patience, encouragement, and grace (especially on our 21st anniversary).

And to our four beautiful children,
You are the living proof that love and connection still wins. KNGU.

How to use this book

This book is designed to be a practical and hopeful guide.

Each chapter follows a rhythm:
three movements designed to engage your
head, heart, and hands.

You don't need to rush.
You don't need to read it all at once.
Some will move straight to the practical sections.
Others will linger in the reflections.
Both are okay.
This guide is meant to meet you where you are.

The following is an invitation to notice, to
remember, and to rebuild a quieter rhythm for
you and those you care for.

OPENING – THE PAUSE

A story with a quiet beginning.
Here, we slow down. We listen.
This section sets the emotional tone and
invites reflection before the research arrives.

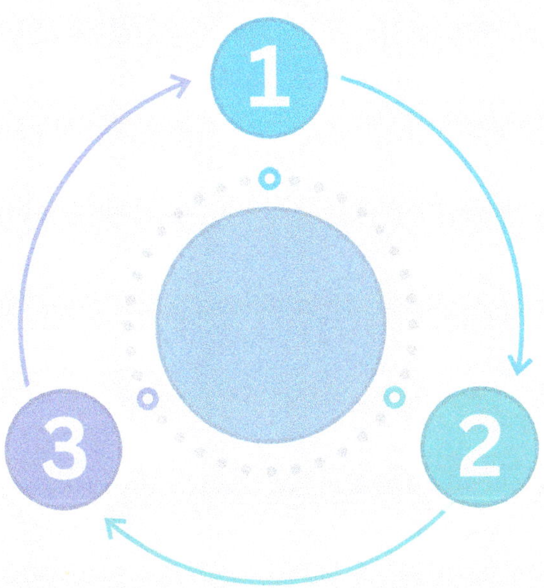

CLOSING – THE RETURN

Gentle integration.
Each chapter ends with reflection –
what this means for you, your family,
your classroom, your community.
It's the place to breathe, connect, and
begin again.

CORE – THE PRACTICE

Where insight meets evidence.
Here you'll find the psychology,
neuroscience, and lived examples
that bring each idea to life, with
Research Spotlights that ground
inspiration in real data.

SUMMARY

AUSTRALIA'S SOCIAL MEDIA MINIMUM AGE LAW – 2024

Establishing a minimum age of 16 for social media accounts, promoting shared responsibility between parents and platforms

The Bibliography for this summary contains the link to a page hosted by the Parliament of Australia and will give you access to:
- *The full text of the Bill*
- *Explanatory Memorandum*
- *Bill Status*
- *Links to Parliamentary debates and committee reports*

 AUSTRALIA'S SOCIAL MEDIA MINIMUM AGE LAW – 2024

Introducing an age threshold (16yrs) for social media, recognising that both parents and platforms have a role in protecting young people online.

WHY IT MATTERS

1 IN 3 AUSTRALIAN TEENS REPORTS POOR MENTAL HEALTH LINKED TO SOCIAL MEDIA USE *(HEADSPACE NATIONAL YOUTH MENTAL HEALTH SURVEY, 2023)*	*The law responds to evidence that early, unregulated social media exposure affects sleep, self-esteem, and identity.* *It's not about banning technology. It's about delaying exposure until young minds are ready.*

WHAT THE LAW DOES

- Requires age 16 minimum for social media accounts.
- Platforms must verify age and restrict under-16 accounts.
- Enforcement by Australia's eSafety Commissioner.
- Significant non-compliance penalties.

WHO IT AFFECTS

NOTE: THE ABOVE IS FOR ILLUSTRATIVE PURPOSES ONLY. THESE PLATFORMS WERE AMONG THE FIRST AFFECTED.

Legislation applies to platforms designed for social interaction and content sharing. Messaging, education, and gaming apps are generally exempt.

A GLOBAL SHIFT

Other nations (including the UK, US, and EU) are exploring similar youth protections. This is more than legislation. This is a step toward digital wellbeing as a human right.

INTRODUCTION

When Screens Go Quiet

Practical Parenting After Australia's Social-Media Age Limit

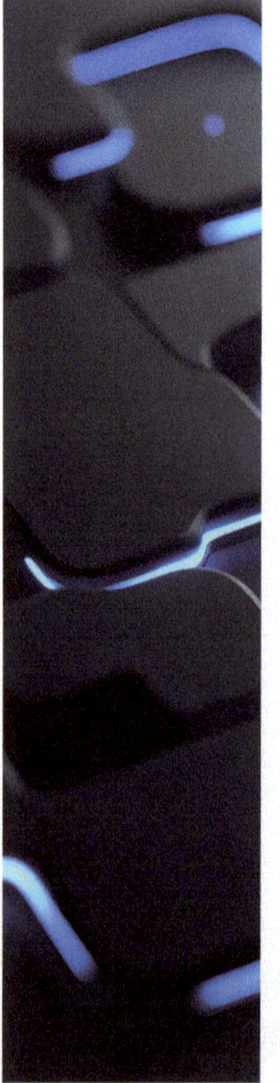

Something unprecedented is happening in Australian homes.

Screens that once buzzed in bedrooms, kitchens, and car rides have gone quiet. Notifications have stopped. Accounts have been restricted. Platforms that shaped how young people socialised, expressed themselves, and found belonging have suddenly been taken away. And in the silence, something else has surfaced.

Across Australia, parents are witnessing heightened emotional outbursts, withdrawal, anxiety, confusion, and anger from their children. For some families, it feels as though everything has unravelled overnight. For others, the ban has simply illuminated challenges that were already simmering beneath the surface.

This is not coincidence.

This is not a parenting failure.

It is the human aftermath of a national decision, one that has asked every household to pause and re-examine how digital life has been shaping the next generation.

A National Reckoning

In December 2024, the Australian Parliament passed the Online Safety Amendment (Social Media Minimum Age) Bill 2024, establishing a minimum age of 16 for social-media accounts (Parliament of Australia, 2024). The legislation (now part of the Online Safety Act 2021) requires major platforms such as TikTok, Instagram, Snapchat, Facebook, and X to take reasonable steps to prevent under-16s from creating or maintaining accounts (eSafety Commissioner, 2025).

This reform, which took effect on 10 December 2025, reflects a broader acknowledgment: that social-media environments have become too powerful, too pervasive, and too unregulated to leave unchecked.

NOTE: This visual represents national trend patterns drawn from Australian youth wellbeing research (ABS, AIFS, Orygen, Mission Australia). It illustrates the growing convergence of mental health distress and digital immersion over time. Figures are indicative and designed to show directional change rather than exact annual prevalence.

For the first time, a national government has formally recognised that the digital ecosystems shaping children's attention, identity, and wellbeing are not neutral spaces. Rather, they are systems designed to capture attention and monetise emotion.

The Online Safety Amendment (2024) seeks to **protect young users from algorithmic designs that prey on developing attention** (Parliament of Australia, 2024).

The Monster Beneath The Behaviour

When screens are removed, many parents expect relief. Instead, they're met with resistance.

Why?

Because for many young people, social media has not just been entertainment, it has been infrastructure: their primary source of belonging, their coping mechanism for stress, their social currency, their mirror for self-worth, their escape from boredom or pain.

When that structure is taken away, what remains is not peace, but exposure to the raw emotional landscape underneath:
- *Anger may be grief.*
- *Withdrawal may be shame.*
- *Defiance may be fear.*
- *Anxiety may be the absence of distraction.*

This is why the ban feels disruptive. It is not simply removing a habit; it is interrupting a formation system that has been shaping young hearts and minds every day for over a decade.

Australian youth data shows rising distress since 2012 among heavy social-media users, with **links to poor sleep, comparison, and low self-worth** (Orygen, 2023; Headspace, 2023; Mission Australia, 2023).

A Moment of Reckoning – And Opportunity

Australia's policy response signals something profound. We are beginning to recognise that digital environments form us, whether we intend them to or not (Parliament of Australia, 2024).

Policy can set boundaries.

Regulation can slow an industry.

But formation…*the deep work of nurturing identity, attention, and empathy*…happens in the small spaces of daily life: around the table, in classrooms, in conversation.

When the screens go quiet, families are left holding the question: **"Now what?"**

This book exists for that moment.

Not to shame parents.

Not to blame young people.

Not to pretend the past decade didn't happen.

Because the monster is real, but it is not unbeatable.

And this moment, disruptive as it feels, may be one of the most important opportunities we've had in a generation to rebuild connection, resilience, and meaning in our homes.

The eSafety framework calls for **shared responsibility across policy, industry, and parents**, noting that **digital wellbeing begins with relationships at home** (eSafety Commissioner, 2025).

Social media platforms were not designed with child development in mind.

CHAPTER ONE

Replacing the Scroll
Why Structure Soothes the Nervous System

When the screens go silent, the house doesn't fall quiet right away. The silence is filled with rustling, sighing, protest...like a room remembering how to breathe. Children pace the edges of it, unsure what to do with time that isn't being directed by pings or playlists. Parents feel it too: that subtle pull to reach, to scroll, to soften the silence.

This moment of unease isn't failure. It's the body recalibrating after years of borrowed rhythm.

Where algorithms once told us when to look, laugh, and react, structure invites the nervous system back into conversation with itself. Researchers at the University of New South Wales describe this transition as a *"re-patterning period"*, the brain's stress circuits spike briefly before settling into calmer baseline activity once predictable routines replace variable digital rewards (University of New South Wales, 2023). This first week is often referred to as *"the storm before the stillness"*.

A 2023 UNSW study found that after families added daily screen-free rituals, **children's cortisol spiked briefly, then dropped below baseline by week four** (University of New South Wales, 2023).

Structure doesn't suppress freedom, it restores safety. Psychologist Stephen Porges calls this the *"social engagement system"*. This is the neural network that allows humans to co-regulate through rhythm, tone, and gaze. When family life regains rhythm (bedtimes that mean something, dinners that happen together, etc), the body reads those patterns as protection (Porges, 2022).

Parents sometimes worry that predictable routines make life dull, but predictability isn't the enemy of joy, it's the soil it grows from. Children play most creatively when the frame around them feels sturdy.

A study from the Harvard Center on the Developing Child found that consistent routines correlate with higher self-regulation and emotional literacy in middle-schoolers. This is evidence that repetition becomes reassurance, not restriction (Harvard 2022).

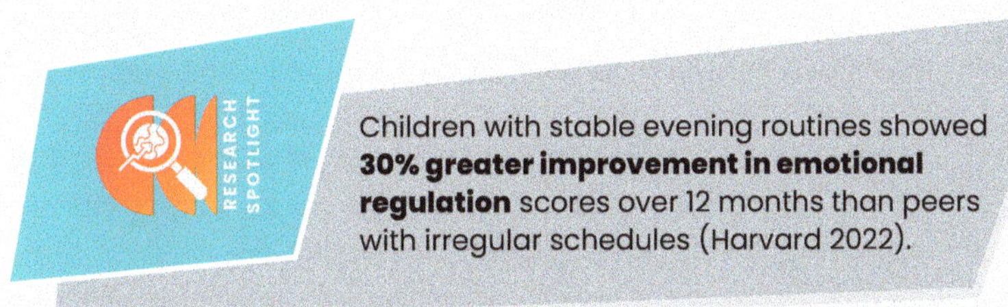

Children with stable evening routines showed **30% greater improvement in emotional regulation** scores over 12 months than peers with irregular schedules (Harvard 2022).

The first days of replacing the scroll are therefore less about subtraction than substitution. This is a process of swapping algorithmic rhythm for human rhythm. Think of it like retuning an instrument...the strings feel tight at first, but the sound that follows carries warmth again.

In 2021, researchers from University College London discovered that adolescents with consistent daily rhythms (sleep, meals, study) showed lower amygdala reactivity, indicating better stress regulation (Henderson et al., 2021).

In simpler terms, "calm" isn't natural. It's a response trained through rhythm.

Platform Native Behaviours Are Key To Driving Engagement

If the first step is recognising how digital life feels, the next is understanding how it works. Behind every swipe, scroll, and notification lies an ecosystem designed to capture attention and convert it into engagement. These are what we call *platform-native behaviours*, patterns so embedded in design that they shape how we see, think, and respond before we even notice. From infinite scrolling to algorithmic cues, every feature has a purpose to keep us returning, reacting, and revealing more of ourselves.

Over the next few pages, we'll explore how these design choices have rewired our habits. This is not to shame our use, but rather to help us see the systems we're swimming in. Once we see the pattern, we can start choosing differently. To ground this understanding, we'll explore six key elements:

 **Scrolling Patterns:** Endless scrolling removes natural stopping points, training the brain to seek constant novelty and making it harder for young people to disengage or tolerate boredom.

 **Content consumption habits:** Short, fast, emotionally charged content conditions attention toward immediacy and reaction rather than depth, reflection, or sustained focus.

 **Platform norms:** Unspoken rules about what to post, like, or ignore quietly shape behaviour by rewarding conformity and punishing difference through social feedback.

 **Visual cues:** Notifications, colours, sounds, and visual badges are deliberately designed to trigger urgency, anticipation, and emotional response, bypassing rational decision-making.

 **The algorithm:** Algorithms learn what captures a user's attention and then amplify similar content, often intensifying emotions, narrowing perspective, and reinforcing identity loops.

 **Native tools:** Features like filters, stories, streaks, likes, and shares are built to turn everyday interaction into performance, linking self-worth to visibility and engagement.

Scrolling Patterns — Dopamine & Reward Loop Effects

Excessive short-form video consumption activates the brain's reward system similarly to addictive behaviours like alcohol or gambling, increasing impulsivity, reducing focus, and impairing emotional regulation.

Research showed that habitual consumption of short-form content (like TikTok/Reels) produces addiction-like brain changes, weakening the ability to find enjoyment in everyday life and impairing decision-making, focus, and sleep quality.

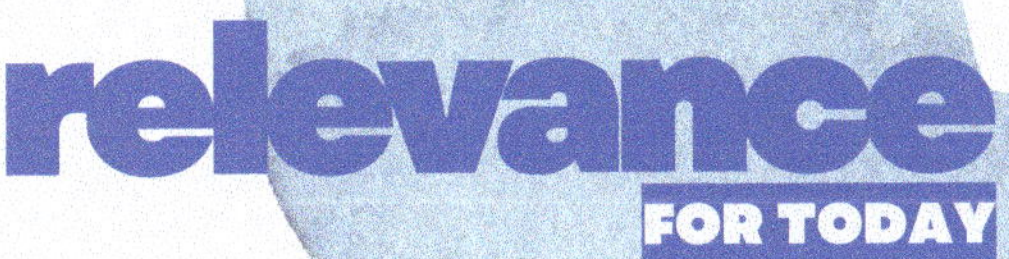

It demonstrates how scrolling patterns create neurological effects that make disengagement difficult and everyday tasks less rewarding.

Study finds short-form video impacts brain reward pathways, increasing impulsivity and weakening decision-making, effects likened to addictive behaviours.

https://www.news.com.au/lifestyle/health/watching-shortform-videos-affects-brain-like-alcohol-study-finds/news-story/76955958bd51b20ace6be9c31fa27823?utm

Content Consumption Habits — Harmful Body Image Feeds

An internal Meta study found vulnerable teens who already felt bad about their bodies were fed eating disorder-adjacent content at much higher rates, with harmful content making up 10.5% of their feed versus 3.3% for other teens.

Teens already struggling with body dissatisfaction saw nearly three times as much harmful, body-focused content in their feeds than their peers, including provocative imagery and judgemental posts.

relevance **FOR TODAY**

This shows how consumption habits on a platform can reinforce negative self-perceptions and emotional harm.

Internal Meta research shows teens with body dissatisfaction saw more harmful image content than their peers.

https://www.reuters.com/business/instagram-shows-more-eating-disorder-adjacent-content-vulnerable-teens-internal-2025-10-20/?utm

Platform Norms - Algorithmic Promotion Of Harmful Content

Algorithmic auditing research found that short-form platforms (Reels/TikTok/Shorts) frequently serve harmful videos to under-18 accounts, with 15% of recommended content deemed harmful to younger viewers, often appearing within minutes of passive scrolling.

general
SUMMARY

Younger accounts encountered unsafe or distressing videos more frequently and quickly than older accounts, sometimes within 3 minutes of passive use, revealing how platform norms and recommendations predispose young users to harmful content.

relevance
FOR TODAY

It illustrates how platform norms aren't neutral but tend to amplify risky or distressing material, especially for younger users.

Study finds accounts assigned to age 13 encountered harmful video content more frequently and quickly than older accounts on major short-form platforms.
https://arxiv.org/abs/2505.11160?utm

Visual Cues - Algorithmic Body & Beauty Feeds

Qualitative studies report that teens often encounter algorithm-generated body-image and beauty-ideal feeds (e.g., "glow up" videos) that promote idealised standards; participants described repeating patterns of seeing fitness and thinness content.

One Year 12 teen described algorithmic feeds pushing daily routines and body goals videos, and others noted that visual cues around beauty and fitness shaped their social comparisons.

This points to how visual cues (repeated imagery of idealised bodies and norms) shape self-perception and internal pressures.

Research with teens reveals persistent exposure to algorithmically recommended body-ideal content and beauty norms.
https://www.mdpi.com/2673-995X/4/3/66?utm

The Algorithm – Harm Pathways & Mental Health

Research on adolescent cyberbullying shows that algorithmic exposure and bystander experiences online can increase suicide risk through a cascade of victimization and internalising symptoms.

Frequent social media use linked to bullying and victimisation correlates with persistent sadness, hopelessness, and increased suicide risk, suggesting that algorithmically amplified social interactions may exacerbate harm pathways.

This shows how interaction patterns shaped by algorithms, not just content, create chains of harm affecting mental health.

Findings indicate that exposure to bullying content online, magnified through platform interaction patterns, correlates with higher internalising symptoms and suicide ideation.
https://link.springer.com/article/10.1007/s42380-024-00269-y?utm

31

Native Tools – Mental Health Support vs Addictive Feedback

Recent Australian research found that while many youths search social media for mental health support, large proportions are deeply concerned about addictive features like infinite scroll and lack of content control.

Half of young people with probable mental health issues reported they sought support online, yet many expressed concern about the addictive nature of platform features and harmful content exposure.

This illustrates how native tools, such as scrolling, endless feeds, and recommendation spikes, can both attract those seeking help and simultaneously expose them to addictive patterns and harmful material.

Research shows young people seek mental health support on social feeds but are concerned about addictive features and harmful content exposure.
https://about.au.reachout.com/blog/new-research-by-reachout-finds-young-people-are-scrolling-their-social-feeds-for-mental-health-support-but-platforms-are-not-safe-enough?utm

What we're witnessing isn't disorder, it's the emotional recalibration that follows years of digital overstimulation.

From Digital Loops To Daily Rhythm

The nervous system loves rhythm because rhythm means predictability. Our ancestors woke with light, ate with community, and rested with darkness. Now, devices interrupt that ancient cadence hundreds of times a day. Each alert is a micro-surprise, a jolt of uncertainty that keeps the body slightly braced. That's why stillness can feel stressful at first, it lacks the artificial beat we've been dancing to.

Dr. Judson Brewer, a psychiatrist and neuroscientist at Brown University, calls this the *"habit loop"* of modern anxiety. It's the cycle of trigger, behaviour, and reward that keeps the brain hooked on distraction (Brewer, 2021).

NOTE: visual created for illustrative purposes only.

Breaking this habit loop requires not punishment, but replacement. What you are doing is creating new cues that lead to calming rewards instead of digital spikes.

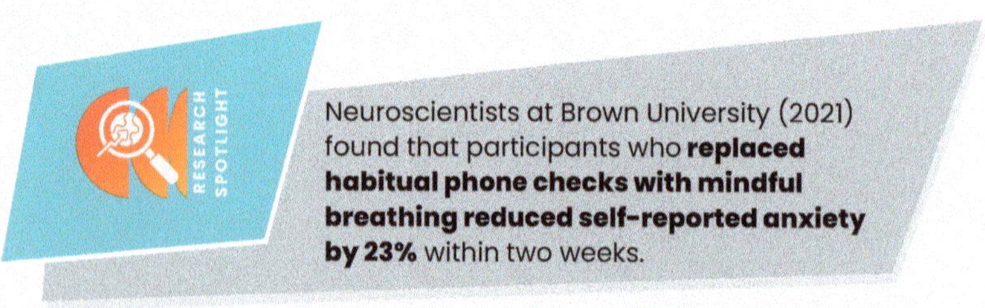

Neuroscientists at Brown University (2021) found that participants who **replaced habitual phone checks with mindful breathing reduced self-reported anxiety by 23%** within two weeks.

When we build new micro-structures (a morning walk before school, ten minutes of shared reading after dinner, etc) we are not just managing time; we are rewiring expectation. Each repeated cue tells the body *"you're safe now; you know what comes next"*. Over time, children internalise that sense of sequence and begin to regulate without prompting.

A family recently shared with me that they began lighting a candle at dinner as a signal that "real life" was starting. At first their teenagers rolled their eyes. Several weeks later, they light the candle themselves. Ritual turns repetition into meaning. The same pattern appears in schools. Teachers who open class with two minutes of quiet breathing or stretching report calmer transitions and improved focus. Monash University researchers measured heart-rate variability (a key marker of calm) among Year 6 students before and after adopting "start-of-day rituals". Within six weeks, variability improved by 18%, indicating greater physiological regulation (Monash University, 2023).

Classrooms using **daily two-minute grounding rituals** recorded **lower behavioural incidents and higher student engagement** scores (Monash 2023).

Building A Daily Rhythm That Works

A simple, flexible daily rhythm may include the following four elements:

MOVEMENT

Physical activity is one of the most effective regulators of mood and behaviour. It does not need to be organised sport: walking the dog, bike rides, backyard games or time at the park all count! For many children, movement first thing in the afternoon reduces conflict later in the evening.

CREATION

Social media consumption is passive. Children benefit from activities where they make something: drawing, music, building, cooking, writing, or even designing a small project. Creation restores a sense of agency that scrolling often replaces.

CONNECTION

Face-to-face interaction rebuilds social skills that have atrophied online. This might look like family dinners, small group activities, youth programs, or time with trusted adults outside the immediate family. Even short, consistent connection matters.

REST

True rest is different from digital escape. Quiet time, reading, reflective practices or simply doing nothing help children relearn how to sit with themselves, a skill increasingly rare and increasingly necessary.

Why Rhythm Becomes Assurance

Predictability frees attention for creativity. When children no longer need to scan for what's next, they rediscover the joy of boredom, which some have suggested is the birthplace of imagination.

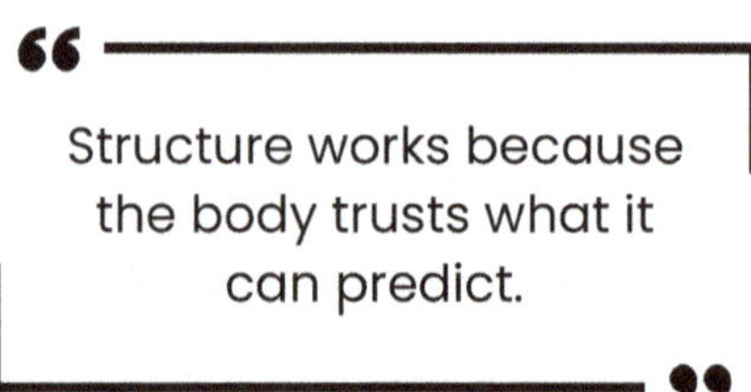

Every family that reduces screen time feels that uncomfortable space first, the stretch between distraction and discovery. But what follows is not emptiness, it's expansion. You start to notice the small sounds. Laughter from the next room, the rustle of someone making toast, the rhythm of your own breath returning. Structure doesn't imprison a child's curiosity, it anchors it! Within routine, freedom becomes safe to explore again. The nervous system, once trained to chase novelty, begins to recognise peace as pleasure.

Psychologists often describe rhythm as a form of love made visible, an invisible promise that the world will keep showing up in the same, kind way. When that promise holds, children learn to trust both others and themselves. A parent who replaces the scroll with steady presence teaches a nervous system to exhale. And in that breath, belonging returns.

Reflection

What times of day are currently the most challenging in our household?

Which unmet needs might be contributing to my child's behaviour?

How do I personally respond to unstructured time or boredom?

Action

Choose one small rhythm to introduce this week (maybe a walk, a shared meal, or a regular check-in) and commit to it for seven days before evaluating its impact.

For many young people, the issue is not defiance, but a loss of orientation.

CHAPTER TWO

Relearning Belonging
Helping Children Rebuild Connection

I've heard it said that belonging begins the moment we feel seen without performance. When we take away the endless scroll, many children discover they don't quite know how to connect without it. The phone has become the social compass, guiding every moment of approval, humour, and attention. Removing it can leave a silence that feels like exile. Belonging, however, is not built through bandwidth. It's built through being known, and that takes practice.

Just as muscles weaken when unused, our capacity for unfiltered presence needs retraining. Researchers at Mission Australia found that nearly half of young people felt *"socially unsure"* after cutting back on screen use, describing awkwardness in face-to-face situations (Mission Australia, 2023). What looked like withdrawal was really a skill gap. Conversation, patience, and turn-taking had atrophied under constant digital mediation.

47% of teens reported feeling **socially unsure post-screen restriction**, highlighting the need for intentional offline practice (Mission Australia Youth Survey 2023).

The removal of social media has not taken away children's desire for belonging. It has simply revealed how much help they need to experience it face to face.

Why Belonging Matters

It's easy to assume connection will automatically return once devices disappear. In reality, it has to be rebuilt through small, repeated gestures, such as eating together, eye contact, shared chores, inside jokes that belong only to your household. Connection thrives where predictability meets play.

Dr. Brené Brown describes belonging as *"the opposite of fitting in...a state where we are accepted for who we are, not who we perform to be"* (Brown, 2017). It's the freedom to show up as yourself, not the version engineered for engagement.

Belonging, as Brown explains, is not a social skill, it's a soul posture. It can't be earned through performance or maintained through perfection. It's the quiet confidence that you are worthy of connection without qualification.

In many ways, our digital culture has blurred that distinction. Young people have grown up in environments where fitting in is measurable, through likes, follows, and algorithms that quantify approval. What was once a process of becoming known has been replaced by being seen.

Local Insights

The result, according to the Headspace National Youth Mental Health Report (2023), is an epidemic of surface-level connection. Teens are reporting that they are *"always connected but rarely known"*. When belonging is replaced by performance, relationships become conditional.

This, and similar other reports, show that children start to monitor themselves through imagined audiences, editing language, tone (even emotion) to match what's rewarded online. But true belonging, the kind Brown describes, doesn't demand editing. It invites presence. It grows in families, schools, and communities where authenticity is modelled, where difference is not just tolerated but welcomed. When that kind of belonging takes root, young people stop asking, *"Am I enough?"* and start asking, *"Where can I give?"*

Social media once offered children a shortcut to reassurance (likes and comments as proof of acceptance). Without those cues, many feel less socially safe, leading to withdrawal or irritability often mistaken for defiance. Coaching connection takes patience and repitition.

41

Teens who spent at least two hours per day in offline group activities such as sport, music, and volunteering showed **40% higher self-esteem and lower social anxiety** (Orygen 2023).

When we replace filtered interaction with genuine attention, we restore the social mirror children need. Real faces reflecting real empathy. The likes and comments that once offered quick reassurance are now replaced with relationships that must do the slower work of being present.

The Science Of Seeing And Being Seen

In the digital age, many children confuse visibility with connection. Likes look like love. Followers feel like friends. But visibility does not equal being known, it's being watched. And when you live mostly through being watched, you forget how to be *with*.

Social neuroscientist Matthew Lieberman calls our social brain the *"default network"*. When we're not focused on a task, the mind naturally turns toward people. Remembering, imagining, and rehearsing connection is what it does (Lieberman, 2013). Constant online distraction keeps that network half-activated. We see faces without feeling them, we scroll stories without sensing their weight.

Prolonged social-media multitasking reduces activation in the brain's default-mode network, **the region that supports empathy and self-reflection** (Lieberman et al. 2022).

When families begin to relearn belonging, they must first relearn slowness. Eye contact is a muscle and so is listening. Dr. Dan Siegel's research on *interpersonal neurobiology* shows that mutual gaze and coherent storytelling can literally synchronise brain waves between parent and child (Siegel & Bryson, 2020). I would go as far as to say that the ancient act of talking around a table is still a biological miracle.

Parent–child conversation that includes storytelling and eye contact **strengthens the child's capacity for emotional regulation and self-awareness** (Siegel 2021).

In schools, teachers see this same pattern. A local primary school I have worked with implemented device-free lunchtimes for its students. After just one week, students reported that games became more inclusive and friendships more stable. Teachers noticed less teasing and more laughter. Evidence suggests that when children aren't performing for an audience, they relax into authentic play.

Schools that implemented two weekly "unplugged hours" saw a **25% drop in reported peer conflict and a rise in cooperative behaviour** (UNICEF 2024).

Belonging isn't a sentiment, it's a practice of attention. Every moment of eye contact, shared joke, or unrushed conversation is a tiny vote for connection over performance. Over time, those votes re-pattern the brain toward trust. It's easy to underestimate these moments - a chat in the car, a walk after dinner or a quiet check-in before bed. This is where real attachment grows. Connection doesn't arrive in grand gestures. It is built in the small, consistent noticing of each other. The child who feels seen daily learns not just to seek belonging, but to offer it. That's how community begins again.

When Connection Slows, Understanding Deepens

When we strip away the noise, what remains is often tenderness, though it can feel fragile at first. Without the quick dopamine of the feed, affection becomes slower, quieter, and much more real. Families rediscover that love is less a feeling and more a series of repeated gestures - a glance across the table, the sound of laughter that isn't being recorded, or the comfort of simply being in the same room.

Belonging doesn't return overnight; it grows like a root system. Unseen for a while, then suddenly everywhere. The silence that once felt awkward becomes fertile ground for shared stories and new traditions. A mother recently told me that she and her teenage daughter started walking the dog each evening after dinner. At first, they talked about nothing, plenty of awkward pauses, phone temptations evident for both. By week three, the conversations flowed. Structure had made space for belonging to bloom again.

Dr. Kristin Neff calls this process *"compassionate presence"* (Neff, 2021). It's the ability to stay open and kind even when emotions run high. When we remain emotionally available instead of disappearing into our screens, we teach our children something profound. Our availability demonstrates that attention, in and of itself, is a form of care. In a world where distraction is constant, choosing to truly notice someone becomes an act of resistance. Research on self-compassion and mindful awareness shows that this kind of presence doesn't just soothe emotion, it also strengthens empathy and emotional regulation in both parent and child. Each time we pause, breathe, and look into our child's eyes instead of our phones, we're rewiring relationship patterns toward safety and trust. Attention becomes love made visible.

A Hopeful Recalibration

While the loss of social media has disrupted familiar patterns, it has also created space for recalibration. Many families are discovering new conversations, deeper relationships and a renewed appreciation for shared time. Relearning belonging takes time. There will be missteps, awkward moments and resistance. Yet, with patient guidance and supportive environments, children can develop social skills that are not only functional, but deeply human. Trust the process, embrace the journey.

Parents who modelled active listening and device-free interaction reported **stronger emotional closeness and reduced family tension** within six weeks (University of Melbourne 2023).

Teens describing family time as "calm and connected" were **2.4× more likely to report good mental health outcomes** than those who described it as "distracted" (Headspace 2023).

Belonging, then, isn't something we enforce, it's something we rehearse. Each time we choose presence over performance, we remind our children, and ourselves, that connection was never lost, only interrupted.

The Irish poet and philosopher John O'Donohue captures this truth in his blessing, *"For Belonging"*. He reminds us that belonging cannot be commanded into being, but rather must be cultivated with tenderness and space for growth. His words invite us to remember that true belonging begins when we allow one another the freedom to become:

> May you listen to your longing to be free.
> May the frames of your belonging be
> generous enough for your dreams
> *(O'Donohue, 2007).*

O'Donohue reminds us that belonging is a rhythm we return to. As we choose patience and curiosity, our families and communities rebuild the kind of connection that lasts.

Reflection

How does my child currently experience belonging?

What social situations seem easiest or hardest for them?

How do I respond to my own social discomfort?

Action

This week, create one low-pressure opportunity for face-to-face connection and follow it with a gentle, curious conversation about how it felt.

Belonging grows where presence meets patience, where children are guided to show up, stumble, and discover their own social courage.

CHAPTER THREE

Boundaries That Build

How Clear, Consistent Limits Create Safety and Strengthen Relationships

Parents often think boundaries will cause conflict. But real boundaries don't create distance, they create safety. They're not punishments, they're promises. When a child knows where the edges are, they can relax inside them.

In the age of endless digital access, the line between freedom and overwhelm has blurred. Children are growing up in a world where every impulse can be instantly met with a swipe, a message, a video. When everything is possible all the time, the nervous system never rests. Setting digital boundaries can feel like swimming against the tide of culture.

But boundaries are not barriers, they are invitations to rest. They signal that home is a place of rhythm, not reaction. When screens go quiet, attention deepens and relationships regain texture. Children may push against boundaries, but this testing is how they learn safety. Each calm "no" from a parent teaches predictability, showing the child that security doesn't vanish under pressure. As Harvard's Center on the Developing Child (2022) found, consistent limits activate neural pathways responsible for emotional regulation and impulse control, strengthening the brain's prefrontal cortex, the seat of focus, empathy, and choice. Boundaries teach the brain to delay gratification, which is the foundation of both discipline and joy. Over time, the very structure that once caused friction becomes the thing a child depends on most, proof that safety doesn't shrink freedom, it steadies it.

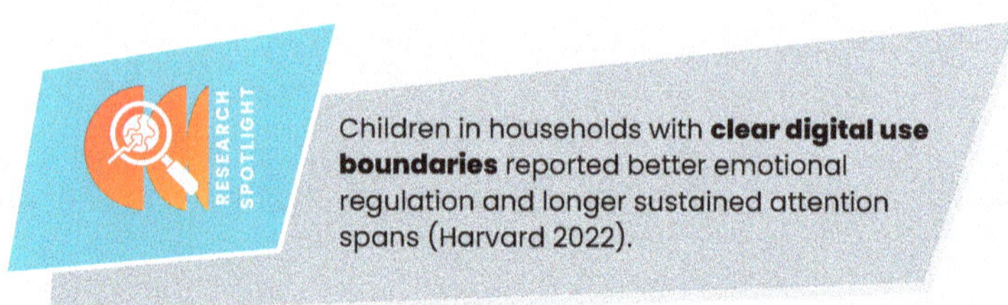

Children in households with **clear digital use boundaries** reported better emotional regulation and longer sustained attention spans (Harvard 2022).

Neuroscience explains why. The prefrontal cortex, the part of the brain that manages impulse control, develops through repetition and gentle challenge. Each time a parent calmly enforces a limit, the child's brain practices self-soothing and internal rule-setting.

Over time, those external boundaries become internal ones. Parents sometimes fear that rules will push their children away, but data from the Australian Institute of Family Studies shows the opposite. Adolescents whose parents maintain firm but empathetic boundaries report greater trust and higher relationship satisfaction (AIFS, 2023).

Boundaries are, in essence, love with a backbone. They say *"I care enough to hold you steady while you learn to stand"*.

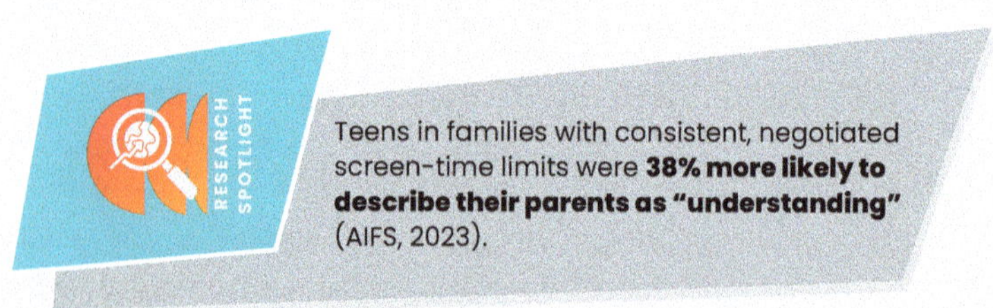

Teens in families with consistent, negotiated screen-time limits were **38% more likely to describe their parents as "understanding"** (AIFS, 2023).

Holding The Line Without Losing Consistency

When parents first introduce new boundaries, friction is almost guaranteed. That's not a sign you've failed, it's a sign your child has noticed. Boundaries make the invisible visible, and visibility is often uncomfortable before it becomes comforting.

Dr. Mona Delahooke, a clinical psychologist who studies childhood behaviour, explains that most pushback isn't defiance but dysregulation. A child testing a limit is really testing for safety: *"Will you still hold me when I'm upset?"* When parents meet protest with calm consistency, the child's nervous system learns that structure and love can exist together (Delahooke, 2021).

Children respond best to boundaries paired with co-regulation, calm tone, predictable response, and repair after rupture (Delahooke, 2021).

In one family I worked with, parents introduced "offline hours" from dinner until bedtime. The first week brought slammed doors and sulks. By the third, those hours became the most peaceful part of their day. The children began playing cards, the parents started talking again. Boundaries didn't shrink their world, they gave it shape. Researchers at the University of Queensland observed similar outcomes when families practiced "digital sabbaths". After a month, children reported feeling *"less rushed"* and *"more in control"* of their time. What began as restriction ended as relief (University of Queensland, 2023).

Families observing one tech-free evening per week reported **improved mood regulation and family cohesion** (University of Queensland, 2023).

Consistency Is Key

Consistency is what turns a boundary into belonging. A limit that changes daily becomes a guessing game; a limit that holds becomes an anchor.

When children trust the edges, they stop testing them so fiercely. Behavioural science calls this *"predictable co-regulation"*, the process by which adult steadiness becomes the template for a child's self-control. It's not just behavioural, it's biological. When a parent remains calm, the child's stress response begins to synchronise, and the nervous system learns to settle more quickly each time.

Harvard's Center on the Developing Child (2022) found that when children experience calm correction instead of punishment, neural pathways in the prefrontal cortex strengthen. This is the wiring behind focus, empathy, and emotional balance.

Every calm response is more than good parenting, it's brain-building. Each moment of steadiness teaches a child that safety isn't silence or control, but connection. Over time, that calm becomes theirs too. This becomes a blueprint they carry into their own relationships, showing that love can hold firm boundaries without fear.

Predictable co-regulation **strengthens executive function and empathy** in developing brains (Harvard Center on the Developing Child, 2022).

The Calm After Consistency

Boundaries work not because they control behaviour, but because they communicate stability. When children know what to expect, they no longer need to scan the environment for danger. Predictability quiets the stress system and frees the mind for learning, play, and curiosity.

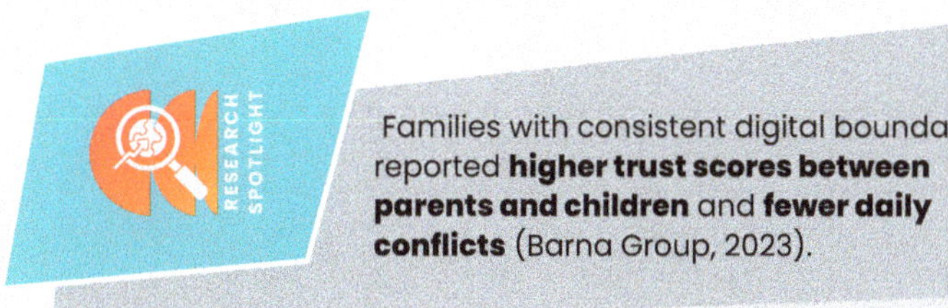

Families with consistent digital boundaries reported **higher trust scores between parents and children** and **fewer daily conflicts** (Barna Group, 2023).

As I have reflected on my journey as a father raising my four children with my beautiful wife, I recognise that our children don't often thank me for the limits we have set in place, but they sleep better, and so do we! That's the paradox of boundaries. They rarely feel good in the moment, yet their benefits unfold in peace that no one can quite name. Every calm limit held is a love letter written in structure. Every "no" said gently becomes a "yes" to emotional safety.

The digital world rewards immediacy, and parenting rewards endurance. Our job isn't to eliminate tension, but to hold it with grace until understanding grows. Boundaries, when done with compassion, don't build walls, they build trust. This trust that builds is what allows freedom to expand without fear. Parenting is the long rhythm of love, the quiet work of staying steady when everything else speeds up. It's patient, often unseen, and sometimes thankless, yet it shapes the emotional architecture of home.

As Kendrick Lamar raps in "LOVE" (2017):

> "Give me a run for my money, there is nobody, no one to outrun me…"

In family life, love isn't about outrunning, it's about outlasting, showing up, again and again, until calm becomes the loudest voice in the room. When your child finally stops arguing and leans into the safety of your consistency, you'll realise that boundaries were never the end of connection, they were its beginning. They are love, practiced slowly, in real time.

Reflection

Which boundaries in our home currently cause the most conflict?

Are our expectations clear, consistent and connected to purpose?

How do I usually respond to pushback? Reactively or calmly?

Action

This week, choose one boundary to clarify or renegotiate as a shared agreement, and communicate it during a calm moment rather than in conflict.

Boundaries aren't barriers, they're bridges of trust. When limits are clear and consistent, they create safety, not restriction.

CHAPTER FOUR

When Behaviour is a Signal
Understanding Mood, Anxiety and Withdrawal

When screens go quiet and a child is reduced to tears, shouting or withdrawal, it can seem like rebellion. More often, it is emotion finding its way to the surface, a child asking to be understood. Our brains are always looking for something steady to rest on. Rhythm tells the body, *"You're safe here."*

Removing digital stimulation can initially feel like yanking away a life raft. The dopamine dips, the body protests, and children often express this through frustration, defiance, or sadness. Psychologists remind us that all behaviour is communication. What looks like resistance is often *"dysregulation"*, which is what happens when the nervous system moves outside its window of tolerance. It's when emotion, stress, or sensory input exceed what the brain and body can comfortably manage. It's not misbehaviour, it's a signal that regulation has been lost and safety needs to be restored (Delahooke, 2021; Siegel, 2020; Harvard Center on the Developing Child, 2022).

Headspace's 2023 National Youth Report found that young people experiencing screen withdrawal exhibited symptoms similar to mild anxiety disorders. But rather than pathology, these reactions signal recalibration.

Screen withdrawal symptoms often mimic irritability, restlessness, and emotional volatility in **temporary nervous system adjustment** (Headspace, 2023).

Parents who recognise this shift as physiological, not personal, can respond with empathy instead of escalation. When we interpret behaviour as data, not defiance, connection stays intact even through conflict. A moment of meltdown, seen differently, becomes a message: *"I'm overwhelmed and I don't yet have words for it."*

Understanding The Science And The Stories Behind The Signals

When children struggle, their nervous systems speak louder than their words. The sigh, the stomp, the slammed door. Each one of these is a message in Morse code asking: *Am I safe? Do you still see me?* Dr. Dan Siegel and Tina Payne Bryson call this the *"downstairs brain."* It's the limbic system that floods with emotion when a child feels misunderstood or threatened. Screens, for all their colour and noise, often keep that system overstimulated. When you remove them, the raw feelings they once numbed begin to surface (Siegel & Bryson, 2020).

Emotional outbursts after screen reduction often mark the **return of natural self-regulation rhythms** rather than behavioural regression (Siegel & Bryson, 2020).

It's why the first weeks of digital reset can feel like living with a stranger. Children oscillate between boredom and agitation, grief and glee. But just as the body detoxes from sugar, the nervous system detoxes from overstimulation. At the University of Sydney, researchers studying digital abstinence found that participants (both children and adults) experienced mood volatility before reaching a state of greater calm and focus around day ten.

Since July 2024 I have had the privilege of working with our State's Health Department, specifically focusing on youth/young adults (and their caregivers) admitted for mental health issues. Where elements of tech addiction are evident, I have found the initial digital reset response to be *emotional turbulence before smooth air.*

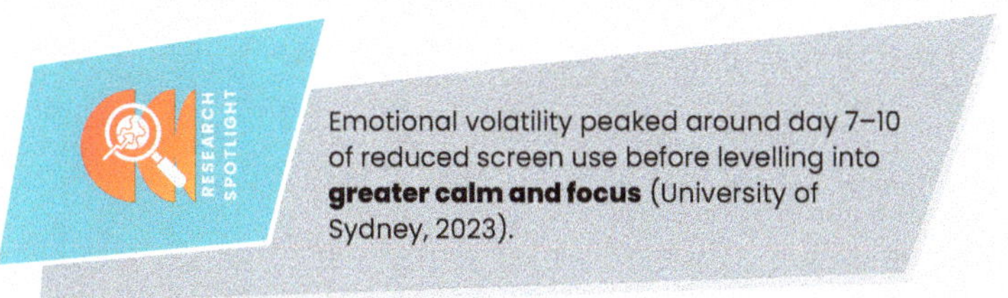

Emotional volatility peaked around day 7–10 of reduced screen use before levelling into **greater calm and focus** (University of Sydney, 2023).

In practice, listening beneath behaviour means slowing down your own reactions first. Instead of meeting a tantrum with logic, meet it with presence. A calm adult body communicates safety more powerfully than any lecture. Behavioural therapist Dr. Mona Delahooke writes, *"Children borrow our calm until they can find their own"* (Delahooke, 2021). That's co-regulation in action. The parent's steady rhythm becomes the child's borrowed heartbeat.

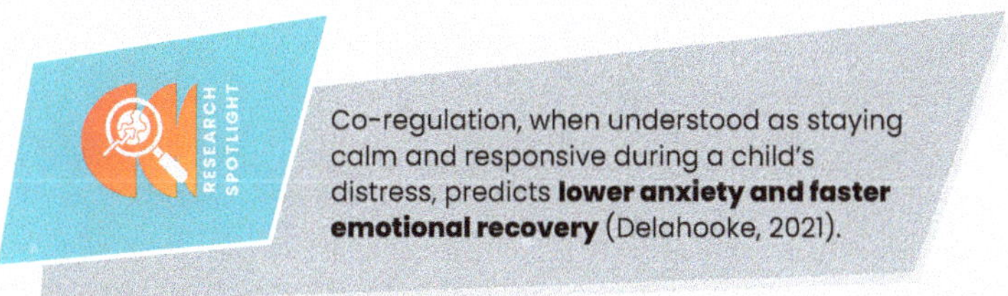

Co-regulation, when understood as staying calm and responsive during a child's distress, predicts **lower anxiety and faster emotional recovery** (Delahooke, 2021).

One of the caregivers I worked with told me she stopped saying, *"Calm down,"* and started whispering, *"I'm right here."* The difference was immediate. The child still cried, but this time, he leaned in instead of away. When children feel seen, behaviour softens.

It reminded me of something I was told during my pre-marital counselling that has quietly shaped not just my marriage, but every relationship since: *no matter what the situation, never say, "I told you so".* Believe me when I say this has been simple but profound advice. It's an invitation to choose empathy over being right. The same truth applies in parenting. When we replace correction with connection, walls lower. Our calm becomes the cue for theirs.

of Australian families are concerned about their young person's mental health

of families talk about mental health weekly with their child

of concerned families don't feel confident seeking professional help

of parents worry about their teen's emotional wellbeing

of teens are diagnosed with either a mental health or neurodevelopmental condition

of teens fail to meet daily physical activity recommendations

NOTE: Figures are based on publicly available Australian youth mental health research and are for informational purposes only. For full context, refer to sources such as McCrindle, Barna, and the Australian Institute of Health and Welfare.

Listening With More Than Your Ears

Every outburst holds information, but decoding it requires stillness. When we react from fear or frustration, we meet dysregulation with more dysregulation. When we pause, we make space for meaning to emerge.

A child yelling, *"You never understand me"* might be saying, *"I'm scared of disappointing you"*. A slammed door might mean, *"I've lost control of something and need you to hold steady until I find it again"*. Calm doesn't mean quiet, it means available. Our nervous systems communicate long before our words catch up. When we stay soft in tone and open in posture, we signal safety through the body before the brain can name it. Parents sometimes say, *"I just want them to listen,"* but children can't listen until they feel heard. Connection always precedes correction.

When families adopt this mindset, behaviour stops being a battlefield and becomes a barometer, a reading of needs, fatigue, and feelings.

Instead of asking, *"What's wrong with you?"* we start asking, *"What happened to you?"* or even, *"What do you need from me right now?"*

Behaviour, seen through this lens, becomes a map back to belonging. The noise of conflict softens into communication. And in the space between reaction and response, relationships deepen.

Reflection

What emotional changes have I noticed in my child recently?

How do I typically respond to emotional outbursts or withdrawal?

Who could support our family if we needed additional help?

Action

This week, choose one low-pressure moment to check in emotionally with your child, focusing on listening rather than fixing.

Adjustment takes time;
patience and presence turn
disruption into growth.

CHAPTER FIVE

Raising Digitally Wise Children
Not Just Digitally Restricted Ones

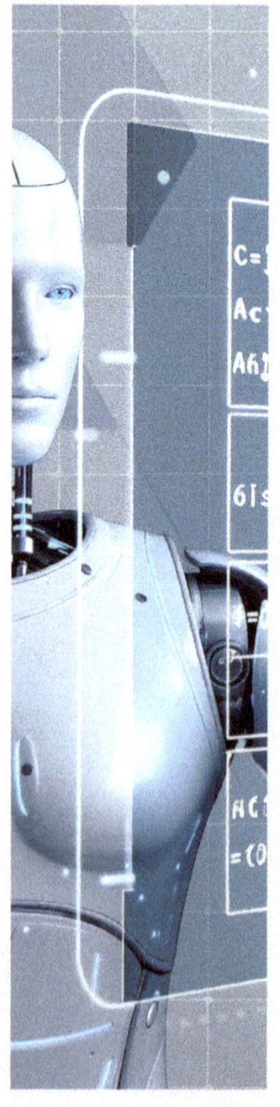

It's tempting to believe that raising digitally healthy children means keeping them offline. But the goal isn't to raise restricted children, it's to raise resilient ones. Our children are growing up in a world where the internet isn't an activity, it's an ecosystem. It seeps into their classrooms, friendships, and imaginations. Screens aren't just tools anymore, they're teachers, entertainers, confidants, and mirrors. For parents, this reality can feel overwhelming: *"How do we guide our children through something that never existed in our own childhoods?"*

Keeping them safe isn't about shutting the world out, it's about lighting a path through it. When parents move from control to coaching, something shifts. The conversation changes from fear to formation, from restriction to relationship. The focus stops being on what's forbidden and starts being on what's forming. Digital wisdom begins when we treat technology not as the enemy, but as an environment, one our children must learn to navigate with discernment and grace. A digitally wise child isn't just avoiding danger, they're learning to recognise manipulation, manage impulse, and make meaning.

UNESCO's Digital Literacy Framework (2024) defines

wisdom as *"discernment in place of denial"* (UNESCO 2024). In other words, we don't need to raise children who fear technology, we need to raise children who understand it.

Digital wisdom develops not through restriction but through **guided discernment and critical thinking** (UNESCO, 2024).

Families that talk about algorithms, advertising, and attention are teaching more than screen rules, they're teaching self-awareness. When a child understands that social media is designed to keep them scrolling, the act of stopping becomes an expression of autonomy. Digital literacy expert Dr. Kristy Goodwin describes this as *"moving from mindless consumption to mindful connection"* (Goodwin, 2023). Children can't unsee manipulation once they've been taught to recognise it.

Building Digital Discernment In Everyday Life

Digital wisdom isn't a single talk, it's a lifelong conversation. It begins when we stop treating screens as the enemy and start treating them as the environment our children are growing up in. You wouldn't drop your child into a foreign country without teaching them the language. In the same way, we shouldn't drop them into the digital world without teaching them how to read it.

Research from Monash University (2024) found that when schools incorporated *"digital reflection"* sessions, guided discussions about online behaviour, students reported feeling more confident and less reactive when confronted with online conflict. The power wasn't in restriction but reflection.

Reflective discussions about online experiences **reduced impulsive responses and improved online empathy** among students (Monash, 2024).

A parent once told me about a ritual she started with her teenage son called *"scroll share"*. Every Sunday night, they would each take turns sharing one thing they saw online that inspired them, and one thing that made them uneasy. There are no lectures, no eye rolls. Just a quiet ritual of curiosity. When she told me this, I could hear the relief in her voice. *"It's the first time,"* she said, *"that I've felt like we're in this digital world together."* That's the shift. The goal isn't control, it's connection. These small rituals make the invisible visible. They show our children that wisdom grows through conversation, not surveillance.

Psychologist Dr. Jocelyn Brewer, who coined the term *"digital nutrition"*, reminds us that technology itself is neither toxic nor benign, it depends on the dose and the context. As she puts it, *"What we feed our minds is as important as what we feed our bodies"* (Brewer, 2018). The more we treat digital life like nutrition (something to be balanced, savoured, and talked about), the healthier our shared online habits become.

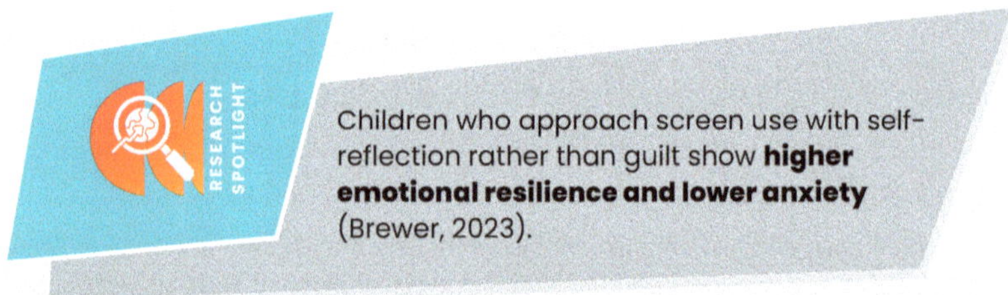

Children who approach screen use with self-reflection rather than guilt show **higher emotional resilience and lower anxiety** (Brewer, 2023).

Parents can model this mindset by verbalising their own digital boundaries. *"I'm putting my phone away now because my brain needs a rest"*. When children hear this, they learn that balance isn't about rules, it's about rhythm. A McCrindle study of Australian families (2023) found that when parents practiced visible digital boundaries, their children were twice as likely to do the same. We teach through what we normalise.

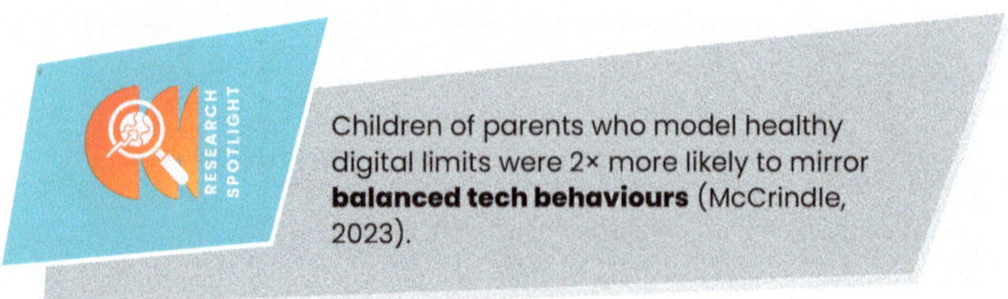

Children of parents who model healthy digital limits were 2× more likely to mirror **balanced tech behaviours** (McCrindle, 2023).

Raising Thinkers, Not Followers

Raising digitally wise kids isn't about keeping them untouched by technology. It's about helping them meet it with awareness, not awe.

When we teach children how to think about what they consume, we give them back their agency. They begin to realise that their attention is not something to be taken, it's something to be given with intention.

Technology will always evolve faster than parenting manuals. But the qualities of curiosity, empathy, and critical thinking, that which makes a child thrive, remain timeless. These are the roots of digital wisdom. True digital literacy isn't just technical, it's emotional and ethical. It's knowing when to connect and when to step back, when to share and when to stay silent. It's the courage to think deeply in a world that rewards speed.

Organisational psychologist Dr. Adam Grant calls this *"confident humility"*, the ability to engage with information without being consumed by it (Grant, 2021). Children who learn to pause, question, and discern, are less likely to fall prey to comparison, misinformation, or manipulation. And perhaps most importantly, they grow up knowing that wisdom isn't about having all the answers, it's about knowing how to ask better questions.

Moving From Fear to Confidence

Parents often ask, *"How do I know if my child is okay online?"* The answer isn't in perfect monitoring, it's in ongoing dialogue.

When a child knows they can bring their digital world into the light of conversation, shame loses its grip. The internet stops being a secret world and becomes an open one. It's easy to approach technology with fear...fear of harm, influence, or losing control. But fear-based parenting often produces rebellion or dependence. Confidence-based parenting, grounded in curiosity and trust, produces discernment. Parents don't need to master tech, just listen, learn, and lead with curiosity. It's time to move from *"technology is dangerous"* to *"technology requires wisdom"*, because wisdom grows through connection, not fear.

Reflection

How do we currently talk about technology in our home — with fear, frustration or curiosity?

What values do we want to guide our child's future digital choices?

Does my own use of technology model wisdom, or distraction?

Action

This week, initiate one conversation focused not on rules, but on how technology shapes attention, emotion and identity.

Freedom isn't doing whatever you want; it's knowing why you choose what you do. This is resilience in a wired world.

CHAPTER SIX

Identity Beyond the Algorithm
Raising Children Who Know Meaning & Purpose

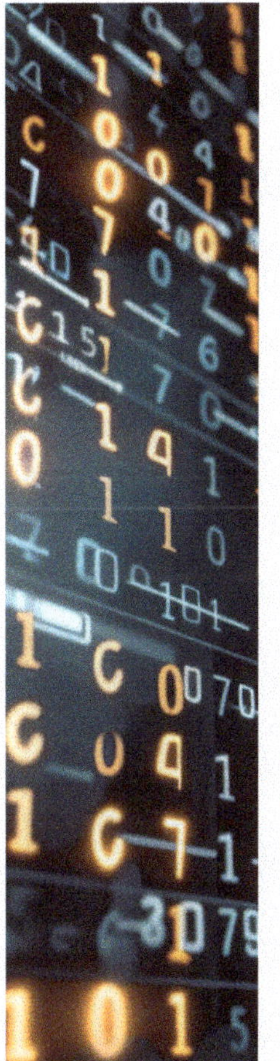

The modern teenager grows up under constant observation. Every photo, post, and reaction becomes part of a public mirror, a curated self reflected through algorithms. It's no wonder so many young people are exhausted by the effort of being seen.

We once learned who we were by looking at the people around us. Our family, our friends, our teachers. Now, identity is often co-authored by strangers. Social media doesn't just reflect, it edits. It rewards certain expressions of self and punishes others through silence. When we lose touch with who we are, the digital world is quick to step in, offering endless versions of ourselves to perform. And if we're not careful, we start to believe them.

Psychologist Dr. Jean Twenge's research shows that teenagers who spend more than three hours per day on social media are significantly more likely to report loneliness, even when surrounded by online "friends". The connection feels endless, but the intimacy is shallow (Twenge et al., 2019).

In this new landscape, belonging has become performance-based, measured in metrics and filtered through approval.

Many young people aren't just trying to connect; they're trying to exist visibly. Yet the more they chase recognition, the less anchored they feel. True belonging, however, begins where performance ends, in spaces where being known matters more than being noticed. Perhaps that's the quiet work ahead for all of us. To help the next generation remember that they are not their profiles, their posts, or their projections. They are the story still unfolding beneath the noise.

Heavy social-media use correlated with **higher loneliness and self-comparison,** even among teens with strong offline support (Twenge, 2023).

When children grow up performing for the algorithm, they begin to mistake attention for identity. Every like becomes a micro-dose of validation. Every pause becomes a potential rejection. The result isn't confidence, it's dependence.

Monash University's 2024 longitudinal data revealed that adolescents who reported fewer daily screen hours but higher engagement in real-world contribution (like volunteering or mentoring) demonstrated more stable self-concept clarity and lower comparison-driven anxiety (Monash, 2024).

Teens engaged in contribution-based activities show **greater identity stability** than those oriented around social-media feedback loops (Monash, 2024).

Parents can't remove the internet, but they can restore perspective. Identity grows best in soil rich with belonging, purpose, and reflection, not constant evaluation.

Helping Children Find (And Keep) Themselves

Identity isn't discovered in a single lightning moment. It's assembled slowly, through relationships, reflection, and trial. Yet the internet teaches the opposite lesson. The lesson often is this: *who we are can be chosen instantly and broadcast globally.*

When a child's identity forms through external validation, it becomes fragile and brittle under the weight of other people's opinions. Developmental psychologist Erik Erikson described adolescence as *"the stage of identity versus role confusion"* (Erikson, 1959). It's when young people experiment with who they are and how they fit into the world. But the algorithm compresses that exploration, rewarding consistency over curiosity. Online, you can't change your mind without losing followers.

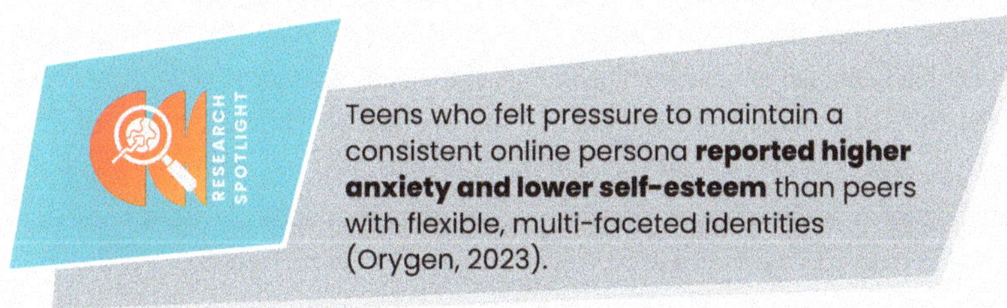

Teens who felt pressure to maintain a consistent online persona **reported higher anxiety and lower self-esteem** than peers with flexible, multi-faceted identities (Orygen, 2023).

Offline, change is normal. Online, it's punished. That's why part of raising grounded kids today is giving them permission to evolve, to outgrow old versions of themselves without shame. Sociologist Sherry Turkle calls this the *"sacred space of pause"*, the reflective gap where the self grows stronger than the noise (Turkle, 2015). Families can create that space by inviting slow identity moments: shared walks, journaling, storytelling, meaningful silence.

In one high school I worked with, teachers introduced a new practice involving ending each week with *gratitude circles* - students sharing one thing they were proud of from the week. Over time, those reflections began shifting from appearance-based to character-based answers. It was the slow untraining of algorithmic identity.

Contribution-oriented teens reported **stronger identity anchoring and greater optimism** about the future (Barna, 2023).

Identity also strengthens when it serves something larger than itself. Volunteering, mentoring, creativity...these are mirrors that reflect purpose, not performance. They remind young people that their value isn't measured in visibility but in contribution.

A Barna Group study (2023) found that young people engaged in acts of service were 2.5 times more likely to describe their sense of identity as *"anchored"* and *"hopeful"*. Service creates a feedback loop opposite to the digital one. Instead of seeking validation through reaction, it builds meaning through participation. When adolescents invest their time in something beyond themselves (helping a younger student, coaching a sport, creating art, protecting the environment, etc), they experience belonging that isn't conditional. Purpose becomes the platform, and contribution the currency. These moments of self-forgetfulness are not losses of identity, they're the way identity matures.

Neuroscience supports this, too. Studies of pro-social behaviour show that helping others activates the brain's reward circuitry while reducing activity in regions linked to rumination and anxiety (Harvard, 2022). In other words, serving shifts focus from *"How am I being seen?"* to *"How can I be useful?"*

When young people find meaning in giving, they stop performing for approval and start participating in community. Their identity becomes less like a brand and more like a bridge, something that connects rather than competes.

That's the paradox of purpose. When we aim our lives toward something larger than ourselves, the self doesn't vanish, it comes into focus. It's the same truth ancient wisdom has always whispered: *we discover who we are by giving ourselves away.*

Key markers of **identity formation** (confidence, independence, decision-making) are **now occurring later** than a decade ago, especially in digitally saturated cohorts.

Researchers note a trend toward extended adolescence, with young people reporting **uncertainty about values, direction and self-understanding** well into late teens and early 20s.

Australian Institute of Family Studies; McCrindle generational research

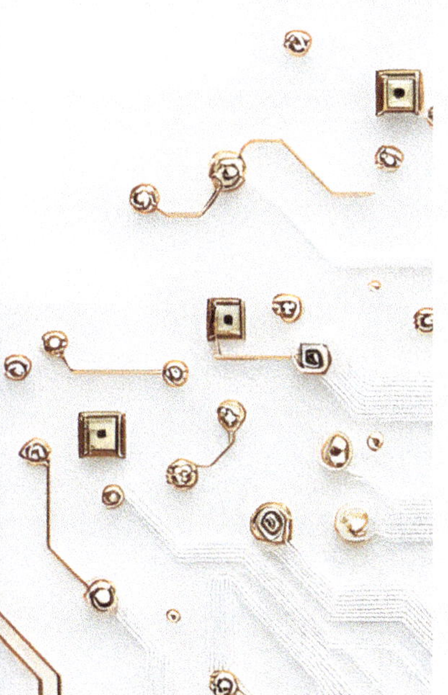

A Deeper, Steadier Sense Of Self

This deeper sense of self is not loud or instantly visible. It does not announce itself through metrics, comparisons or constant updates. Instead, it forms quietly, through experiences of boredom that invite creativity, through frustration that builds resilience, and through relationships that are sustained without performance.

When children stop measuring themselves against a scrolling feed, they gain space to listen inwardly. They start to notice their own preferences, limits, and values, not to display them, but to live them. This inner awareness becomes a steadying force through disappointment, exclusion, or uncertainty.

As identity depends less on approval, relationships grow calmer and more generous. Children can stay present in conversations, disagree without panic, and contribute without fear of being unseen. Parents support this growth not by giving answers, but by creating space for reflection.

Shared routines, unhurried conversations, and steady expectations become the quiet scaffolding where identity matures. Over time, children raised in such environments enter digital spaces not searching for worth, but carrying it, grounded, resilient, and less shaken by the noise around them.

The Self That Stays

When we remove the noise, what remains is the quiet hum of who we've always been. Children discover it in moments of wonder, sketching late at night, helping a younger sibling, getting lost in music or sport. Identity reveals itself not through performance, but through absorption, the times they forget to check who's watching.

Parents can nurture this by naming character over image. Saying *"I love how kind you were"* instead of *"You looked so confident"* shifts the affirmation from appearance to essence. Through practices like this, children learn that who they are matters more than how they appear. Dr. Kristin Neff calls this *"self-compassion"*, the art of treating ourselves as we would a loved one. When children learn to meet failure with curiosity instead of shame, their sense of self becomes resilient rather than reactive (Neff, 2021).

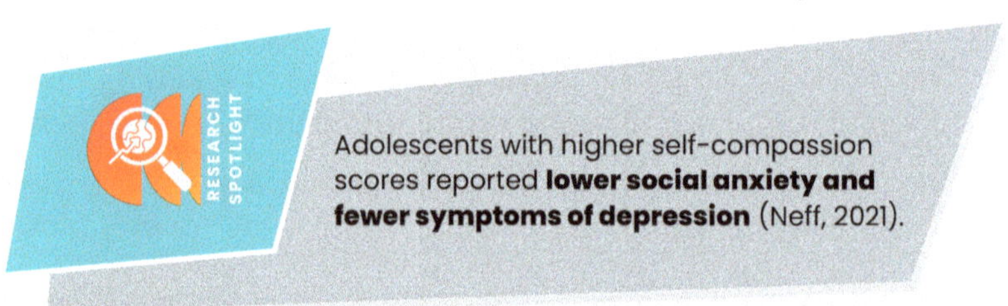

Adolescents with higher self-compassion scores reported **lower social anxiety and fewer symptoms of depression** (Neff, 2021).

Our goal is not to raise children who never doubt themselves, it's to raise children who know where to return when doubt arises. If home is a mirror of acceptance rather than evaluation, they will always find their way back. Identity built offline has weight.

One way to approach the implementation of the legislation this book is focused on is as an encouragement to explore identity held by relationships, rituals, and the rhythm of daily life. The digital world may reflect fragments of who our children are, but only belonging and purpose can hold the whole picture. Could it be that this moment we are living through currently is asking us to help a generation remember that being seen isn't the same as being known?

Reflection

What messages about worth and success might my child have absorbed online?

How do I affirm identity in our home — through words, time and trust?

What practices help our family slow down and reflect?

Action

This week, speak one intentional affirmation to your child about who they are, not what they do, and notice how it lands.

When building up your children with words of affirmation, say something that anchors their identity beyond performance.

CHAPTER SEVEN

It Takes A Village Again
Schools, Community and Shared Responsibility

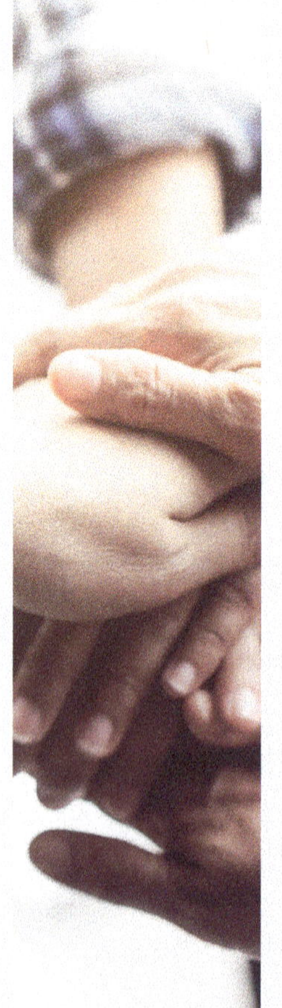

The myth of modern parenting is that we're meant to do it alone, yet no generation in history has raised children in such isolation. Our ancestors had extended families, neighbours, and shared routines. There were aunties who noticed moods before they became meltdowns, uncles who fixed bicycles and built confidence, neighbours who showed up with meals when life got heavy. Their presence wasn't perfect, but it was consistent. It gave children a web of belonging strong enough to hold their growing edges.

Today, many parents are trying to replace an entire village with a single exhausted household, wondering why the task feels impossible. The invisible labour of community once expressed through watchful eyes, shared wisdom and laughter between generations has been replaced by silent scrolling and self-comparison. Screens connect us more widely than ever but leave our relationships thin - stretched across distance and starved of depth. Children need more than followers; they need a network of trusted adults who see them, guide them and reflect who they're becoming. Caregivers, too, need shoulders beside them, people who remind them they don't have to hold it all alone. Raising children was never meant to be a solo act; it was always meant to be a shared rhythm.

This expression of healthy community helps children build identity and resilience. Emerging research supports this. Structured intergenerational and community-based activities, which engage youth with adults beyond their parents, are linked with improvements in wellbeing and reductions in social isolation (Campbell et al., 2024). This evidence suggests that when young people are connected with a broader web of supportive adults, mentors, neighbours, teachers, and community volunteers, their emotional resilience gains ballast that no single household can provide.

This is not surprising when you remember that one pair of hands cannot hold a child. It takes overlapping, imperfect care. It takes a community that notices, nurtures, and guides. The work of raising resilient children isn't about perfection, it's about participation. When support is shared, so is strength.

We were never meant to raise children inside echo chambers. Children were meant to grow up surrounded by people who see them from different angles and still call them worthy. That's how belonging gets layered. It's one relationship at a time.

Sociologist Robert Putnam famously wrote about the decline of *"social capital"*, the invisible glue that binds communities (Putnam, 2022). His later work found that shared activities like communal meals, volunteering, and faith-based gatherings predicted stronger wellbeing and lower anxiety among children and teens. The antidote to isolation isn't just self-care, it's *shared* care.

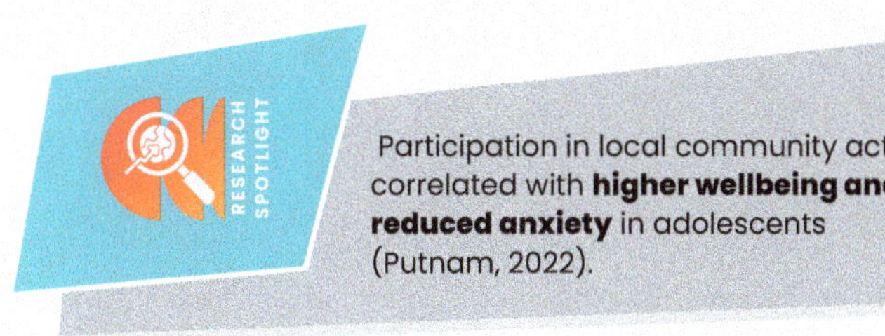

Participation in local community activities correlated with **higher wellbeing and reduced anxiety** in adolescents (Putnam, 2022).

Rebuilding The Modern Village - Schools As Frontline Partners

Schools are among the first places where the effects of social media withdrawal become visible. Teachers notice changes in attention, social dynamics and emotional regulation. Many Australian schools are already adapting, integrating wellbeing programs, restorative practices and social skills development into daily life. Parents can strengthen this partnership by:

- *Communicating openly with teachers or wellbeing staff;*
- *Sharing observations from home;*
- *Seeking guidance when concerns arise.*

Approaching schools as allies rather than authorities fosters shared understanding and consistent support for children across environments.

If a child's world is only as big as their household, their safety net will always feel fragile. My experience tells me that when the circle widens to include the expression of community we are exploring here, resilience grows exponentially. When my children reached the age 13, I had a dozen of the significant others in their world write letters to them calling all the attributes they see that make them uniquely who they are. I have often found my children reading through these letters at different times, often during significant moments of trial and tribulation.

The Harvard Center on the Developing Child (2022) describes this as *"the architecture of resilience"*. Children need at least one stable, caring relationship beyond their parents to buffer stress and foster adaptability. That second adult doesn't replace the parent; they reinforce the foundation.

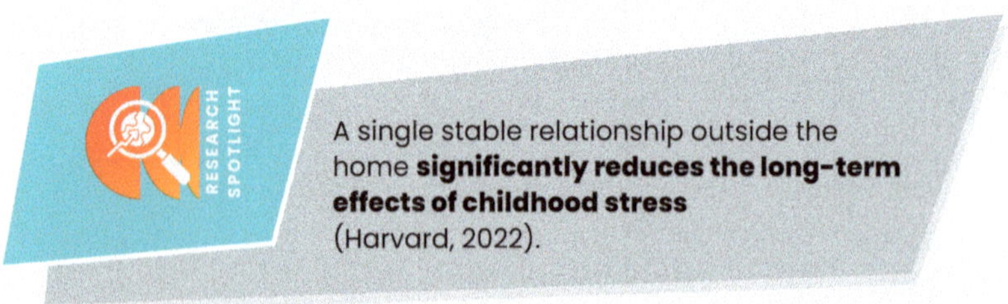

A single stable relationship outside the home **significantly reduces the long-term effects of childhood stress** (Harvard, 2022).

Communities that thrive aren't necessarily wealthy, they're woven. They have shared rituals: markets, morning greetings, after-school chats. Connection happens in the spaces between bus stops and book clubs, in the quiet hellos that tell a child *"you belong here"*.

Neighbourhoods can do this too. When families share supervision, meals, or playtime, children learn that support isn't scarce, it's social. This cooperative care model reduces burnout for parents and teaches empathy to children.

McCrindle's 2023 research on Australian Family Wellbeing found that parents with consistent social support networks reported half the levels of parenting fatigue compared to those without.

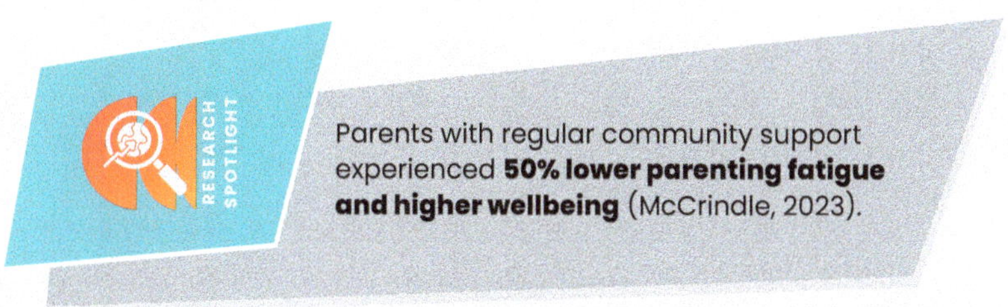

We can't outsource connection to technology or policy, it grows from proximity, practice, and presence. The modern village begins not with big systems but with small, deliberate choices: waving to the neighbour, asking the teacher how they're doing, making space for one more at the table.

Returning To Each Other

The truth is, our children don't just need us, they need us together. They need to see adults cooperate, care, and show up for one another. That's how they learn what belonging feels like.

Community doesn't erase hardship, it makes it bearable. When one parent is tired, another can step in. When a teacher burns out, a mentor can lift a child's confidence again. When a neighbour waves, listens, or simply smiles, that small act stitches another thread in the social fabric.

Communities with higher social cohesion showed **lower rates of youth anxiety and improved life satisfaction** (University of Melbourne, 2023).

And it's this fabric, woven from small gestures of shared care, that science keeps confirming matters most.

There is strong evidence that community-based and mentoring organisations play a vital role in supporting young people in ways families alone cannot. Through mentoring, they enter a wider circle of care: adults who model steadiness, listen without judgement, and create a sense of safety that stretches beyond the home.

Research in youth mental health shows that these relationships strengthen social skills, nurture wellbeing, and ease isolation by offering something algorithms never can, genuine presence (Silke et al., 2025).

Mentoring isn't about advice so much as accompaniment, walking beside, not ahead. Globally, programs like *Big Brothers Big Sisters* demonstrate that sustained, relationship-based support helps young people stay engaged in school, build healthier friendships, and develop confidence that lasts well into adulthood (BBBSA, 2025).

Australian studies echo this. Intergenerational and community mentoring foster resilience and create spaces where belonging is not performed, but lived (Hatzikiriakidis et al., 2021).

Children and teens flourish within a fabric of shared care. Community fills what single households cannot, offering connection, belonging, and steady adult presence that strengthens both courage and character. When we widen the circle of care, we do more than protect the next generation.

We help them remember they were never meant to grow alone.

Reflection

Who currently supports our family in raising our children?

Where might we need additional partnership or guidance?

How do we model help-seeking and collaboration?

Action

This month, identify one community connection (school, sport, youth group or wellbeing service) and take a small step toward deeper engagement.

We are not just
navigating a transition,
we are shaping the adults
our children will become.

A Hopeful Way Forward

The digital world promises connection, yet what our children crave is continuity - people who stay when the feed scrolls on. They need adults who respond with warmth, not metrics.

The disruption of social media has been real and, at times, painful. Yet within it lies hope: a chance to rebuild lives that are slower, more relational, more human. Across communities, families are rediscovering shared meals, unhurried conversations, and the simple act of presence. Raising children has never been a solo task; it has always taken a village. What's changed is our awareness of how deeply we need one another.

When families, schools, and neighbours work together, children gain more than safety, they gain examples of cooperation, care, and resilience. Each act of reconnection protects not only children, but culture itself. The strength of a society is measured by the steadiness of the hands that hold its young. This journey won't be perfect. There will be fatigue and missteps, but also growth, healing, and quiet moments of rediscovery. Healing never happens alone; it happens when the village hums again.

By choosing relationship over isolation, wisdom over fear, and community over control, we shape the kind of adults our children will become, grounded, attentive, and unafraid of stillness.

Thank you for choosing connection in an age of noise. There is reason to hope. You are not walking alone.

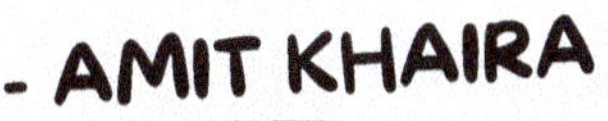

References

Summary – Australia's Social Media Minimum Age Law

Parliament of Australia, Online Safety Amendment (Social Media Minimum Age) Bill 2024.
<https://bit.ly/SocialMediaMinimumAgeLaw>

References

Chapter 1 – Replacing The Scroll

Brewer, Judson A. Unwinding Anxiety: New Science Shows How to Break the Cycles of Worry and Fear to Heal Your Mind. New York: Avery, 2021.

Brown, Judson A. Unwinding Anxiety: New Science Shows How to Break the Cycles of Worry and Fear to Heal Your Mind. New York: Avery, 2021.

Harvard University, Center on the Developing Child. Building the Core Capabilities for Life. Cambridge, MA: Harvard University, 2022.

Monash University. "Start-of-Day Grounding Rituals and Student Engagement." Monash Educational Neuroscience Review, 2023.

Orygen Youth Mental Health. Structured Routines and Adolescent Calm: A National Report. Melbourne: Orygen, 2023.

Porges, Stephen W. Polyvagal Safety: Attachment, Communication, Self-Regulation. New York: W. W. Norton, 2022.

UNESCO. Digital Wellbeing Framework: The Global Report. Paris: UNESCO Publishing, 2024.

University of New South Wales (UNSW). Digital Wellbeing Study: Family Rhythm and Cortisol Regulation. Sydney: UNSW Press, 2023.

References

Chapter 2 – Relearning Belonging

Brown, Brené. Braving the Wilderness: The Quest for True Belonging and the Courage to Stand Alone. New York: Random House, 2017.

Headspace Australia. National Youth Mental Health Report. Melbourne: Headspace, 2023.

Lieberman, Matthew D. "The Default Mode Network and Social Cognition." Social Cognitive and Affective Neuroscience17, no. 2 (2022): 153–66.
Mission Australia. Youth Survey Report 2023. Sydney: Mission Australia, 2023.

Neff, Kristin. Self-Compassion: The Proven Power of Being Kind to Yourself. New York: HarperOne, 2021.

Siegel, Daniel J. The Power of Showing Up. New York: Ballantine Books, 2021.

UNICEF. Digital Wellbeing Schools Pilot. Geneva: UNICEF, 2024.

University of Melbourne. Family Attention and Emotional Closeness Study. Melbourne: University of Melbourne Press, 2023.

References

Chapter 3 – Boundaries That Build

Australian Institute of Family Studies (AIFS). Teens, Trust, and Technology Use. Canberra: AIFS Publications, 2023.

Barna Group. Family Trust Index 2023. Ventura, CA: Barna, 2023.

Delahooke, Mona. Brain-Body Parenting: How to Stop Managing Behavior and Start Raising Joyful, Resilient Kids. New York: HarperCollins, 2021.

Harvard University, Center on the Developing Child. Predictable Co-Regulation and Executive Function. Cambridge, MA: Harvard University, 2022.

Lamar, Kendrick. "LOVE." Featuring Zacari. DAMN. Top Dawg Entertainment, 2017.

University of Queensland. Family Digital Sabbath Study. Brisbane: University of Queensland, 2023.

References

Chapter 4 – When Behaviour Is A Signal

Delahooke, Mona. Brain-Body Parenting: How to Stop Managing Behavior and Start Raising Joyful, Resilient Kids. New York: HarperCollins, 2021.

Harvard Center on the Developing Child. Foundations of Lifelong Health Are Built in Early Childhood. Cambridge, MA: Harvard University, 2022.

Headspace Australia. National Youth Report 2023. Melbourne: Headspace, 2023.

Porges, Stephen W. Polyvagal Safety: Attachment, Communication, Self-Regulation. New York: Norton, 2022.

Siegel, Daniel J., and Tina Payne Bryson. The Whole-Brain Child: 12 Revolutionary Strategies to Nurture Your Child's Developing Mind. New York: Random House, 2020.

Siegel, Daniel J. The Developing Mind: How Relationships and the Brain Interact to Shape Who We Are. 3rd ed. New York: Guilford Press, 2020.

University of Sydney. Digital Abstinence and Emotional Regulation Study. Sydney: University of Sydney Press, 2023.

References

Chapter 5 – Raising Digitally Wise Children

Brewer, Jocelyn. Digital Nutrition: Building Healthy Tech Habits for Life. Sydney: Digital Parenting Press, 2023.

Goodwin, Kristy. Dear Digital, We Need to Talk: A Grown-Up Guide to Technology and Relationships. Sydney: HarperCollins Australia, 2023.

Grant, Adam. Think Again: The Power of Knowing What You Don't Know. New York: Viking, 2022.

McCrindle Research. Australian Family Digital Balance Study. Sydney: McCrindle, 2023.

Monash University. Digital Reflection Project: Classroom Empathy and Self-Regulation. Melbourne: Monash University, 2024.

Orygen Youth Mental Health. Digital Engagement and Wellbeing Report. Melbourne: Orygen, 2023.

UNESCO. Digital Literacy Framework. Paris: UNESCO Publishing, 2024.

References

Chapter 6 – Identity Beyond The Algorithm

Barna Group. Anchored Identity Study 2023. Ventura, CA: Barna, 2023.

Canberra Department of Education. Schools Reflection Pilot Report. Canberra: ACT Government, 2023.

Erikson, Erik H. Identity and the Life Cycle. New York: International Universities Press, 1959.

Monash University. Identity and Contribution: The Adolescent Longitudinal Study. Melbourne: Monash University, 2024.

Neff, Kristin. Self-Compassion: The Proven Power of Being Kind to Yourself. New York: HarperOne, 2021.

Orygen Youth Mental Health. Youth Identity and Social Media Report. Melbourne: Orygen, 2023.

Turkle, Sherry. Reclaiming Conversation: The Power of Talk in a Digital Age. New York: Penguin Press, 2015.

Twenge, Jean M. Generations: The Real Differences between Gen Z, Millennials, Gen X, Boomers, and Silents - and What They Mean for America's Future. New York: Atria Books, 2023.

References

Chapter 7 – It Takes A Village Again

Barna Group. Five Adults Effect Study 2023. Ventura, CA: Barna, 2023.

Harvard University, Center on the Developing Child. The Architecture of Resilience. Cambridge, MA: Harvard University, 2022.

Hatzikiriakidis, Katerina, Sally Robinson, and Anne Graham. Intergenerational and Community Mentoring: Supporting Children and Young People's Wellbeing and Belonging. Lismore, NSW: Centre for Children and Young People, Southern Cross University, 2021.

McCrindle Research. Australian Family Wellbeing Report 2023. Sydney: McCrindle, 2023.

Putnam, Robert D. Our Kids: The American Dream in Crisis (10-Year Update). New York: Simon & Schuster, 2022.

Twenge, Jean M., Gabrielle N. Martin, and W. Keith Campbell. "Decreases in Psychological Well-Being Among American Adolescents After 2012 and Links to Screen Time During the Rise of Smartphone Technology." Journal of Adolescence 79 (2019): 44–58. https://doi.org/10.1016/j.adolescence.2019.02.009

UNICEF. Community Connection and School Wellbeing Program. Geneva: UNICEF, 2024.

University of Melbourne. Social Cohesion and Youth Wellbeing Study. Melbourne: University of Melbourne Press, 2023.

About The Author

Amit Khaira is an educator, storyteller, and social innovator with over twenty-five years of experience working alongside young people, families, and communities across multiple continents. He is the Founder and CEO of NXT Move Plus 8 LTD, an Australian charity helping youth, young adults and families across multiple sectors navigate modern life with wisdom, resilience, and hope.

Amit's work bridges education, theology, and social impact, grounded in the belief that connection, not control, transforms lives. His own journey through hardship, faith, and renewal continues to shape his empathy and his conviction that there is no story (or person) beyond redemption.

He holds degrees in Business, Education and Theology, including a Master of Theological Studies from the University of Divinity, where he received the Vice Chancellor's Scholar Award.

Amit lives in Perth, Western Australia, with his wife Skye and their four children. Together, they are committed to helping the next generation rediscover what it means to be present, purposeful, and deeply human in a distracted world.

Something unprecedented is happening in Australian homes.

The noise has stopped.
The scroll has slowed.
And in the quiet, families are finally hearing what was drowned out.
In 2025, Australia became the first nation to introduce an under-16 social media ban, marking a global turning point in how we understand technology, childhood and connection.

When Screens Go Quiet explores the emotional, relational and cultural shifts unfolding in its wake. Blending story, psychology and fresh research, Amit Khaira offers a hopeful roadmap for parents, educators and communities learning to navigate this new terrain.

This is not a book about restriction, but restoration, about rediscovering presence in a world addicted to performance and rebuilding the rhythms that make us human again. In a time when everything feels urgent, *When Screens Go Quiet* is an invitation to slow down, listen deeply, and remember what really matters.

Amit Khaira is an educator, speaker and community leader with over two decades of experience working with young people and families across Australia and around the world. He leads NXT Move +8 LTD, supporting youth and young adult communities throughout Oceania and beyond. Amit lives in Perth, Western Australia, with his wife and their four children, who continue to shape his conviction that when screens go quiet, life has something important to say.

WWW. NXTMOVE .ORG